REAL ESTATE INVESTING

Learn How to Flip Houses,
Invest in Real Estate and
Gain Passive Income
in Rental Properties

Table of Contents

Introduction   **V**
Flipping vs. Buy and Hold   **1**
   Flipping vs. Buy and Hold   2
How to Make Money by Flipping   **7**
   The Basic Process of Flipping   7
   Types of Renovations   9
   Building a Flipping Team   12
How to Invest in Buy and Hold Properties   **19**
   The Basic Buy and Hold Process   19
   Choosing a Rental Property   21
   Securing Financing   23
   Finding Tenants   28
   Setting Rents   31
Conclusion   **37**

Introduction

I want to thank you and congratulate you for purchasing the book, "Real Estate Investing: Learn how to Flip Houses, Invest in Real Estate and Gain Passive Income in Rental Properties".

This book contains proven steps and strategies on how to generate passive income by investing in real estate.

***Real Estate Investing* will teach you how to dominate the real estate market by:**

> Helping you decide if flipping or buy and hold is the best real estate investment strategy for you.

> Learning how to flip houses even if you don't have a lot of money.

> Learning how to generate rental income by buying and holding rental property.

> And more!

Thanks again for downloading this book, I hope you enjoy it!

CHAPTER 01

Flipping vs. Buy and Hold

Real estate investment has become increasingly popular among investors as a way of generating passive investment. Real estate represents a more substantial asset compared with stocks, bonds and other financial instruments. In addition, the value of real estate does not fluctuate as much and provides more predictable returns for a particular level of risk. There are many other benefits you can enjoy from investing in real estate. These include the following:

> Since property is a real asset, it has an intrinsic value. This makes it a good hedge against inflation since real estate's value does not erode over time. After all, people will always need property and there is only a limited supply of it.

> Since real estate holds its value over time, it makes a great long-term investment. Investors

who are concerned that they may not get the returns they want from stocks and bonds can park their capital in real estate without fear that they will lose their investments. Even if property values should decline in the short-term, they will eventually rebound again in the long-run.

Real estate can be used to secure financing for other investments. If you need capital, you can borrow against the equity in your property. Since you are putting up your real estate as collateral, it is easier to borrow money and you can even use part of it to pay off your mortgage.

When you have rental properties, you have the option to live in them during times when they are not occupied and producing rental income, or use them for some other purpose.

Flipping vs. Buy and Hold

When it comes to generating income from real estate, there are two basic strategies – flipping or buy and hold. Which one to use depends on your financial goals: do you want a recurring income or a relatively quick return on your investment?

'Flipping' refers to a strategy in which an investor buys property with the intention of reselling it when its value appreciates. This can be due to increases in its price as a result of market forces or as a result of capital improvements and renovations undertaken by the owner. Thus, flipping can be a short-term strategy in which you only hold the property for a few months or a longer-term one in which you unload after completing renovations.

Generally, there are two types of properties that are bought by flippers – homes and rental properties such as apartments that can be purchased at below market value because the owners are in dire financial straits or 'fixer-uppers' with issues regarding their condition that need to be addressed in order to increase their value.

In order for flipping to be successful as an investment strategy, the investor needs to have capital that he can afford to have tied up until the property is ready to be sold. He should keep in mind that once he invests capital in renovating a property, it is tied up and may result in cash flow problems. In addition, there is no guarantee that the investor will be able to quickly find a buyer for the property once it is ready to be sold.

The buy and hold strategy, on the other hand, involves holding on to the property and managing it in order to generate income from it. This is generally in the form of rents that are paid by tenants for the use of the property. The main downside of this strategy is that it requires a lot of time and effort to effectively manage real property. A lot of investors who do not have the time or skills to do so must hire someone to manage the property for them, and this can cut into the income the real estate generates.

For example, the investor will have to screen tenants to find ones who are trustworthy and capable of paying the rent on the property. Once the tenants are installed, the investor will have to manage the property to keep them happy. For example, he will have to ensure that the facilities are in good working order, and that the property is secured against theft and vandalism.

If the investor is able to bear these responsibilities, however, the rental income the property can generate will ensure they are well compensated as long as the property remains occupied.

Which Strategy to Use?

Unless the investor is quickly flipping properties, both strategies involve capital being tied up with no way to quickly liquidate the assets. This would not be a problem if the property is part of a diversified investment portfolio with stocks and bonds that can be sold in order to meet cash flow problems; but if the property is the primary investment, the investor has to decide if they have the tolerance to assume the risks of property ownership.

Another consideration is the skill level of the investor. He needs to be able to find distressed properties whose value can be increased. He also needs to have the ability to manage the property himself in order to maximize the returns he gets.

For those who are adopting a short-term flipping strategy, it should be noted that there are transaction costs that can eat into profits, such as financing, closing and brokerage fees. This can affect the amount of profit the investor earns from his capital. Thus, he has to consider if the can complete enough transactions within a year or other investment period in order to earn a sufficient return once all the transaction fees are taken into account.

To summarize, deciding between flipping or a buy and hold strategy depends on what your financial goals are, as well as your financial situation. If you want to enhance the returns that you are getting, a short-term transactional flipping strategy may be appropriate. On the other hand, if you are planning to build wealth, holding onto real estate long-term may be the better strategy, since it is a real asset that can be used to not only finance other investments but also eventually sold once the market values go up.

CHAPTER 02

How to Make Money by Flipping

I f you've decided to flip real estate, you should prepare yourself for the financial and emotional costs of implementing this investment strategy. Flipping will require a lot of time-consuming hard work on your part, and you will have to exercise a great deal of patience since it may take some time before you see any returns.

The Basic Process of Flipping

The first step is to consider if you have sufficient capital to invest in flipping a house. Keep in mind that you will not only need to have enough to buy the property but also to pay for the necessary renovations. If you don't have enough, then you will either have to borrow money or look for investors who are willing to fund you.

Alternately, you can go into partnership with other people who will either provide the funding or with whom you can pool resources. If you choose to do so, you will have to decide how the funding and the work will be shared, and of course, how the profits will be allocated once the property is flipped.

Next, you'll have to find a property that is undervalued. These days, with the housing market recovering, this can be challenging, but if you're creative enough, it can be done. For example, you can place ads on craigslist inviting people to sell you their property. You can put up so-called 'bandit signs' asking distressed property owners to sell you their distressed property.

If you are willing to do a little more work, you can search public records to find abandoned properties, and then contact the owners with an offer to buy. If you are willing to work with a real estate agent, you will probably be more successful since they will know more about which neighborhoods have distressed properties whose owners are eager to sell.

Once you've found a property and closed the deal for it, you will have to start undertaking renovations. Unless you have substantial experience in performing house repairs, you will need to find people to help you. Of course, the goal is for you to eventually learn enough to be able to do it on your own or supervise people who will do the actual repair work.

To make the house more sellable, when you're performing renovations, keep the eventual owners in mind. For example, if you are in a neighborhood with schools nearby, the buyer will probably be a family man or woman with young children. Thus, you should make sure that there are sufficient bathrooms for both children and adults. If the neighborhood is mostly occupied by residents who are middle-aged or elderly, you can make the home friendlier for their needs. For example, you can add wheelchair or access ramps, as well as make the front entrance more accessible from the street without the resident having to climb up stairs.

Another way you can make the home more attractive to buyers is by providing information about what went into its renovation. For instance, you can include before and after photos in the listing, so the buyer will appreciate just how much work went into it. You should also stress how the home was upgraded from its original state to a more contemporary one.

After you have renovated the property, your agent may tell you that you can sell it for more if you wait a while. In this case, you can generate income from the property by renting it out on a short-term basis until you are ready to flip.

Types of Renovations

If you are renovating a house in preparation for flipping it, one of the most important things is to have the right mindset. When owners renovate a house, they do so with an eye towards making their home the best it can be, and as a result, they often end up overspending. Thus, if they put their home up for sale, they often end up realizing less than they spent on repairs.

As an investor, you have to estimate just how much to spend to ensure that the house is salable, but without losing money on the deal when it comes time for you to flip the property.

The basic repairs that you have to do are those to ensure that any wear and tear, and damage is repaired, as well as to ensure that it is livable. For instance, any leaks on the roof have to be patched, the faucets in the bathrooms should not be leaky and the walls have to be clean and in good shape.

In addition to the basics, you will also have to ensure that the house has the amenities that potential buyers would expect based on the neighborhood it is located in. In a wealthier neighborhood, for instance, the house should have air conditioning and other features that are common to properties located there.

It should be noted that these types of repairs don't add value to the house but simply bring it up to a standard level that would be acceptable to buyers. When you invest this money, you are unlikely to get your investment back fully, but it will at least ensure that the house can be sold for the same amount that other houses in the neighborhood would go for.

Here are the other types of renovation projects that will help add value to the property:

Curb appeal is defined as how attractive a house looks when viewed from the sidewalk. Undertaking renovations that add curb appeal may not necessarily boost the price of the house when you flip it, but will certainly ensure that it sells faster. Something as simple as a new coat of paint on the outside of the house or a freshly mowed and cared-for lawn can greatly add to the curb appeal of the property.

Major renovations are those that are seen as the most desirable projects to undertake, since they greatly add to the price of a house. Examples of these projects include remodeling of bathrooms and kitchens, new windows and new siding. Since these are practical features that home buyers would be looking for, once you resell the property you can realize as much as 80% of your investment.

Preferential renovations are those projects that can result in you being able to resell the house for a premium, depending on the neighborhood and the preferences of the buyer. An example of this type of renovation project is a home theater. While you can advertise this as an added feature and charge a premium above what the price would normally be for the house, it might be difficult to find a buyer. Undertaking this type of renovation may be appropriate if you are flipping houses in an upscale neighborhood where price is not that much of a consideration.

Building a Flipping Team

Due to the complexities of flipping houses, no one person can do it alone, and the most successful flippers assemble teams of specialists to help them. Each of these experts will help you handle various aspects of the flipping process.

Estate Agent

As we already discussed, a real estate agent will help you find properties that have the potential to be flipped and resold for a profit. However, they can provide you with more help than that. For example, they can advise you as to which type of renovation project you should undertake to ensure that you could realize the maximum profit on the house. They can also help you to resell it more quickly. They typically take around 5% commission once the property is sold, but the services they provide will more than make up for it.

Estate Attorney

There are a lot of legal ramifications that you should be aware of when flipping a house, in order to stay out of trouble. A real estate attorney can advise you as to how to conduct your flipping activities properly in order to stay within the bounds of the law. In addition, they will help you draft the legal documents that you need to ensure that sales and re-sales are closed legally.

General Contractor

While you can probably do most of the basic repairs yourself, you will need the advice of a contractor to complete more complex ones. You will likely need a team of specialists including carpenters, plumbers, electricians, and so on. The contractor will help you find the people you need, supervise the work, and ensure that any building permits needed are secured. As with an estate agent, the contractor typically charges a certain percentage of the total cost of the work as his fee.

Certified Public Accountant

A CPA can help ensure that you not only pay the correct taxes on your house flipping activities, but that your tax burden is minimized. In addition, they can advise you on the right way to structure your business as well as how to declare what you've earned. IRS regulations regarding real estate investments can be complicated, so you want a CPA who can help you navigate them on your team.

Insurance Agent

Insurance is one of those expenses that seem unnecessary, until you actually need it. An insurance agent can advise you as to what coverage you need in order to avoid liability, as well as protect your investment in case of unforeseen emergencies. In addition, state law may require you to have certain types of policies or face penalties. An insurance agent will not only ensure that you have the coverage that you need, but also help you get them at the most reasonable rates.

Securing Financing

Unless you have a ready source of capital on hand, you will likely need to find funding to finance your flipping activities. Fortunately, there are ready sources of financing that you can tap, even if you have a low credit score.

Hard Money and Private Money Lenders.

This is the quickest and easiest way for flippers who are just starting out to get the money they need. A hard money lender sources money from a group of individuals and lends it out while a private lender may be a single person who loans money directly.

There are actually lenders who specialize in lending money to house flippers and base the amounts they lend on the after repair value of the house, rather than on how experienced the flipper is. They are short-term loans that are usually extended for no more than 12 months since most flipping transactions are completed within that time frame, although some lenders may extend loans for up to 36 months.

It should be noted that the amount loaned is intended to cover both the cost of buying the property and the renovations. This means that you may need to put up some money to cover the shortfall. For example, let's say that you want to flip a property that's worth $300,000 and you estimate that renovations will cost $50,000. If the APV of the property is $500,000 and the lender will only allow you to borrow 65% of that, then you will only get $325,000; thus, you will need to put up $25,000 to complete the repairs before the house can be flipped.

Another important consideration is that the loan not only comes with a high interest rate (typically around 8% to 12%) but also that the borrower will have to pay 'points' to secure the loan (around 4% of the loan amount). These fees will not be charged upfront and will be added on to the amount of the loan to be repaid once the house is resold. Thus, you should figure the cost of the loan into your budget and adjust accordingly.

To qualify for a loan, you should be able to present documents such as a contract of sale and a property assessment, as well as your recent tax returns and bank statements to attest to your financial state. In addition, you should have a credit score of not lower than 600 and a debt-to-income ratio that is not too high. Individual lenders may require other qualifications.

You can easily find hard money lenders online by doing a Google search or using online directories. If you have contacts within the real estate community, you can ask for recommendations as to which ones they use.

Crowdfunding

Once you've successfully completed your first flip, you can try seeking financing from this source. Crowdfunders are a group of people who pool their funds to lend money to flippers. The main advantage of using them is that you can get approved very quickly (in as little as three to five days). Depending on the crowdfunder, you can borrow a certain percentage of the purchase price of the property or the ARV, whichever is lower.

However, the terms offered by crowdfunders are similar to those of hard money lenders, with similar qualifications, although some platforms may require more stringent requirements. You will also need to have a credit score of no less than 600 and not have been foreclosed or declared bankruptcy within the past two years as well as having a debt-to-income ratio that is no higher than fifty percent.

Bank Loans

Once you've been in business for a while, you should approach a bank for financing since they are the cheapest source of funds for business. First time house flippers are unlikely to be approved for a loan, although you can try approaching a bank if you have good to excellent credit. Typically, however, banks only lend to those who have been in business for at least two years.

In addition, you should register your business and prepare a business plan to show the loan officer.

Keep in mind that banks usually do not lend money to individuals for business. You will also have to factor into your plans the longer approval time, since it may take from one to three months before you are approved.

You will also not be financed for the entire purchase price of the property. Generally, banks will only loan you a certain percentage of the price of the property, i.e. 65 percent. Thus, you will still have to find funding for the remaining 35% as well as the expenses for repair and renovation. On the other hand, you will enjoy interest rates of around 3% to 5%, as well as a longer loan term.

If you are approved, the bank will typically extend you a secured line of credit rather than a straight loan. This is beneficial to you since you will only draw the funds that you need and pay interest on them, rather than on the full loan amount. In addition, there are some banks that may be willing to extend an unsecured line of credit in order to pay for the renovations.

Investment Partner

This is another good choice for beginning flippers. Generally, partners will provide you with start-up money so that you can make down payments on properties, as well as starting repairs. To ensure that you will not experience difficulty running your business, find a partner who is willing to fund you, but has no interest in getting involved with the actual flipping.

There are a number of ways to find an investor. You can get in touch directly with investors who are known to finance flippers and other start-ups, but make sure that you are ready with a business plan and other documents needed when you make your presentation. You can also try joining an investment club, if there is one that is active in your area.

Once you find an investor, be sure to consult with an attorney to draft a partnership agreement. This agreement should cover the amount of investment the investor will provide, how profits will be shared as well as how liabilities and debts will be handled.

You should also not undertake any long-term agreements with a particular investor until you are sure that you work well together. After finishing your first flip together, evaluate your partnership and decide if you want to continue.

CHAPTER 03

How to Invest in Buy and Hold Properties

I f you are interested in generating an income from real estate investments or you believe that the market is down and you will not get the returns you want from flipping, you can choose a buy and hold strategy. When you buy and hold a house, you rent it out in order to make money from it. You can buy a home that is already in good condition or choose a fixer-upper that you can refurbish. In the case of the latter, you may choose to rent out the house part-time until property values go up and you can flip it.

The Basic Buy and Hold Process

The first step in the buy and hold investment strategy is to find a property in a desirable neighborhood. In order to make it attractive to tenants as well as potential buyers, the area should have easy access to schools, health care, shops and other amenities. You can ask a real estate agent to help you find properties as well as to determine the amount of rent you can charge.

Once you have located a property and renovated it, if necessary, you have to decide how you will rent it out. If you intend to maintain it as a rental property, you can rent it to tenants on an open-ended basis, meaning they can stay as long as they continue to pay the rent. If you intend to sell it eventually, you can lease the property, which will require the tenants to vacate once the term of the lease has expired.

One option you can consider is a lease option or lease purchase agreement. In the former, the tenant has the right but not the obligation to purchase the property before the lease expires. In the latter, the tenant is obligated to buy after occupying it for a certain period. In both cases, the tenant pays you an option fee, which you will keep whatever action they may decide to take.

Once the property is occupied, you will have to actively manage it. This means that you will ensure that the property remains in good shape at all times, and that you will undertake any repairs that are required. You will also need to address any concerns that your tenants may have. You can perform this function yourself, or hire somebody to do it for you, who may or may not live on-site.

When you are setting rents, it is important that they are enough to generate a positive cash flow. This means that the rent should be sufficient to cover all of the expenses required in managing the property, while leaving you with enough to serve as your profit. Remember that there is a wide range of expenses associated with managing a property, including the cost of any mortgages or loans you may be paying off, insurance premiums, and taxes.

Choosing a Rental Property

When choosing what rental properties to buy, there are a number of important criteria that you have to keep in mind. We have already mentioned the neighborhood the property is located in as well as easy access to schools and other amenities. Here are some other criteria that you should keep in mind:

Average rents in the area: This is an important consideration since it will affect your profitability. Is the average rent enough to cover your expenses and ensure that you have enough left for a profit? If not, can you charge more without deterring tenants from renting in your property?

Employment opportunities: Areas where it is easy to find work will naturally attract more tenants. In addition, having a major business in the area will probably raise property values, and may be a signal for you to consider unloading your investment.

Crime: This is a major concern for tenants so if the area is considered unsafe, you should definitely avoid it. Apart from looking at police presence in the area, you can also look out for indicators such as petty vandalism that may indicate the property is undesirable.

Amenities: What are the amenities in the area? Is there easy access to parks, malls, groceries, movie theaters and other leisure activities? In addition, you should look at how easily you can get to the area using public transportation. Are there public transport hubs near the property?

New developments: If there is a lot of new construction going on in the area, it is probably a growth area with lots of potential for you to charge high rents. On the other hand, you should also consider if the developments will hurt property values in the neighborhood, i.e. if they will cause the loss of amenities that will make it a less attractive place to live.

Property taxes: Paying property taxes will naturally impact on your profits so you want to know what the local rates are. However, this may not be a consideration if you intend to hold on to the property for the long-term.

Vacancies and listings: If there are a lot of listings in a neighborhood, it may signal that the area is undergoing a seasonal fluctuation and that conditions will eventually correct themselves, or that the neighborhood has become undesirable. You should also look at the vacancy rates since low rates mean that you can charge higher rents to tenants.

Securing Financing

As with flipping, unless you have a lot of capital available, you will need to find financing for your buy and hold properties. Unlike borrowing for flipping, however, you will need to borrow money long term, since you are not going for a quick return on your investment. Consider that you will have to use the income you generate to service the loan.

Your Financing Options Include:

Federal Housing Administration loans

FHA loans are mortgages provided by private lenders but insured by the Federal Housing Administration. The borrower shoulders the cost of the mortgage insurance, which makes the loan more affordable. While you can qualify for an FHA loan even with less than perfect credit, you will need a credit score of at least 580 to qualify for a mortgage with a down payment of just 3.5 percent; otherwise, you would have to pay a 10% down payment.

However, since the loans are intended for home-owners, you will have to live in the house. But you can get a loan to buy up to a fourplex, which allows you to live in one unit and rent out the rest.

Private Money

The main advantage of using private money lenders is that you can get the money to acquire the property quickly. Once you've bought it, you can then refinance the property to pay off the hard money loan and then start using it to generate income.

Alternately, if you have already established contacts in the investment community, you can look for one that will extend you a trust deed loan. This loan will cover both the cost of acquisition and any renovations necessary to make the property more attractive to tenants. However, it's usually difficult to convince a private lender to extend such a loan to you on your first deal, and you will probably need to have some successful transactions under your belt before you can approach them. However, if you have a sound business plan that you can present, it would not hurt to try.

Angel Capital

If you have family or friends who have a significant amount of savings that they can lend you, you can approach them and ask for a loan or offer to go into partnership with them. Of course, even if they are willing, you should treat the investment in a professional manner and make sure to have everything in writing, as well as establishing terms such as repayment and profit sharing.

You can also look for someone with capital who will go into partnership with you. However, it is important that you agree that he will be the financier and you will be the 'industrial partner' – that is, you will do all the work. Of course, you will report to him about the results of his investment, but otherwise, he will stay away from the day-to-day management of the properties.

One thing you should avoid, however, is using different partners for every investment. This can cause you some problems later on when it comes to accounting for the profits and the ownership stakes.

Roth IRA

If you have money stashed away in a self-directed Roth IRA, you can use it to invest in real estate. In fact, investing in real estate using retirement savings has become an increasingly popular alternative to traditional options such as stocks and bonds.

However, you should consult with a financial adviser to ensure that your investments are in order to avoid the loss of the account's tax-deferred status. For example, the account owner must hire an administrator to handle the day-to-day business of managing the property since they are prohibited from doing any work on it, and all income generated by the asset (i.e. rents or the proceeds from sales) must be placed directly back to the IRA account.

No-Money Down Deals

This is a financing method that can be successful if the seller agrees to it and they still have a decent amount of equity in their property. The way it works is that you come to an agreement with the seller as to how much you will give them for their property. Then you provide them with a promissory note promising that you will pay them the money by a specific time frame. Alternately, if the seller is motivated to sell off the property, they may provide you with a loan to buy it.

Of course, the main disadvantage of this type of deal is that the seller remains on the original mortgage. Thus, there is a risk that the bank could foreclose if the seller does not continue servicing the loan. In addition, buying the property on a subject to the original financing basis means that the due on sale clause will be activated.

Mortgages

This is the most challenging method of financing real estate investments and you should ensure that you are thoroughly prepared before you approach a bank or mortgage lender. In addition, you should have a good to excellent credit score and a good financial profile. However, you should be prepared to wait for some time before you hear whether or not you are approved and have a contingency plan in case you are turned down.

Another consideration when seeking a bank loan for real estate investments is that you will need to provide a down payment for every property you seek a loan for as well as reserves in an account for mortgage payments. Generally, you will be asked for at least a 20% down payment as well as six months of reserves.

There are also other costs that you should take into account, such as mortgage insurance, appraisal fee, origination fee. In addition, you may need to pay for title insurance, although in most cases the seller shoulders it. The title company may also require you to pay recording fees and a closing fee.

If you choose to work with a mortgage broker, you should make sure that they understand real estate investing. A broker will help you find a loan from among their chosen list of lenders. If they do not understand real estate, they may have problems finding the right loan for you. However, if you find the right one, he can even help you find a lender who will provide finance for multiple investment properties.

You can also consider approaching smaller local banks in the areas where the rental properties are located. They may be more open to extending loans to investors since they have a stake in the economic health of the area.

Finding Tenants

When it comes to finding tenants, it is important that you use a variety of sources. Keep in mind that people looking for a place to rent will look at both online and offline sources during their search, so you have to advertise in as many venues as possible.

The first place to start is by placing ads in local papers. This is a good way to find tenants who are familiar with the local community, making it more likely they will be long-term renters. The best time to advertise is during the weekends, since this is when most people read the classified ads looking for rentals. At the same time, however, ad rates are at their highest so you should aim to produce an ad that is as concise as possible while still providing all the necessary information to potential tenants.

A more affordable alternative would be bulletin boards in churches, supermarkets and bus stops. However, you should be careful in choosing where to place your flyers since you don't want to attract cranks who will prank call your contact numbers as well as undesirable tenants. You can also place 'For Rent' signs on the front of the rental property with a contact number that is clearly readable from the curb.

If you want to widen your search, you can list on sites such as craigslist or Trulia. There are also sites that cater to specific states, if you would want to limit potential tenants only to those living in a particular area.

Another good alternative is using social media such as Facebook and Twitter. You can announce vacancies by posting a status update or list on the Facebook marketplace, as well as sending out tweets that include links where people can learn more about the rental property.

If you are willing to invest some money, you can ask a realtor to list your vacancy. In exchange, the realtor will typically charge around a month's rent as their commission, although this can vary. However, the main advantage of using a realtor is that they will screen tenants for you and send you only those who are genuinely interested in renting and are trust-worthy. Of course, you will still have to meet with them in order to make your decision, but at least you are more or less assured they will not be problem tenants.

Finally, if there is a vacancy that you simply need to fill, you can offer incentives to prospective tenants such as a discount on rent, a month's free rent or even a free TV. And you can write-off the TV as a business expense, so you can offset the cost.

Once you have a list of applicants who have con-tacted you, download or create a rental application for them to fill up. This application will provide you with basic information about them that you can use to make background checks and credit checks. To help ensure that the tenant is serious, you can also charge a non-refundable fee to cover the cost of making these checks.

If there are any terms and conditions you are imposing on tenants, you should include this in the application form so the applicant will know what you do and don't allow. This is particularly important if you are requiring tenants to shoulder extra costs such as requiring them to have rental insurance or pay an additional security deposit, as well as if you are requiring any restrictions such as not allowing pets on the premises.

Make sure that the application requires applicants to provide the names of previous landlords as well as character references. This is the quickest and easiest way of eliminating undesirable tenants, since their old landlords may report problems to you that they did not report to the authorities.

When you initially meet with them to give the application form, ask them to provide you with a valid ID, and a photocopy if possible. The ID should have a photo so you can confirm that it really belongs to them. If they have a car, you should write down their license plate number so you can look it up and provide further confirmation of their identity.

You can hire companies such as SmartMove to conduct your background checks. In addition, the applicant should provide you with permission to access their credit report, since this will indicate if they have the capability of paying their rent.

One important thing to keep in mind is that you should not discriminate against certain applicants. By even appearing to do so, you open yourself to lawsuits by applicants that you passed over. This is why a written application form is important, since it allows you to justify your decision based on business reasons. You and any employees you have should also be familiar with fair housing laws that prohibit you from discriminating on the basis of gender, religion, race or national origin, physical or mental disability and familial status. Depending on the state your rental property is located in, you may also be prohibited from discriminating on the basis of sexual preference.

Setting Rents

There are a lot of factors that go into determining how much rent you can charge to tenants. The most obvious one, of course, is your expenses and your profit: what amount can you charge that will cover all your costs and still provide you with cash flow? Among the expenses to account for are the mortgage payments (if any), maintenance and repairs and vacancy costs.

What other considerations should you keep in mind when setting rents?

The Average Rents in the Area

Unless your rental property is an upscale one with premium amenities, you should set your rent at more or less the same level as the average. If it is too high, unless there is something extra that you can offer tenants to justify the higher price tag, they will not be interested. On the other hand, if it is too low, many reputable tenants will also be deterred from seeing your rental because they believe there may be something wrong with it.

If possible, you should visit other rental properties in the area, to see what they are going for and to compare their amenities and features with what you are offering. This will give you an idea of what you can charge for your rental, and adjust the level accordingly in order to compete.

The State of the Economy

A poor economy can favor you since people may lose their homes and be forced to rent, increasing demand and allowing you to increase your rent. On the other hand, you should also consider the capability of potential renters to pay, since they may be interested in cheaper rentals.

The Attractiveness of the Property

Depending on the amenities and the features available, you may be able to charge higher rents. For example, properties with more bedrooms and closets are more desirable, and thus, you can set higher rents for them. Here are some of the other factors to consider:

The scenery. Does the window of the property look out onto a green lawn or a dingy empty lot? More attractive views mean higher rents.

Square footage. Properties with bedrooms that have a higher square footage can charge more.

Level. If your property is an apartment, you can charge more for units on higher floors. However, if the property does not have an elevator, higher units above the third floor are less desirable since it is too tiring to go up and down the stairs.

Layout. Those apartments that are laid out in a 'railroad' style with the rooms in a line with entrances at either end, are seen as less desirable than those with other layouts.

Features. A balcony and more windows will allow you to charge higher rents since they make apartments and houses more desirable.

The Season

People typically look for rentals in the summer, because they would prefer to move during the warmer months, and this is also when school is out. If you only intend to rent out your rental property on a short-term basis, you should try to schedule your leases so that they would expire during the summer. This would allow you to maximize your rental income while avoiding vacancy since you will likely be able to find another tenant once the old one moves out.

Finally, when setting rents, keep in mind that you would rather attract desirable tenants than undesirable ones. Even if you have to lower the rent a bit to attract a good tenant, it may be worth it if they will take care of your property and pay on time. Even if you know you can charge a particular tenant a higher rent, it may not be worth it if they will give you problems and bother the other tenants.

Conclusion

Thank you again for purchasing this book!

I hope that this book was able to help you to learn how to start making money from real estate investments.

The next step is to start practicing what you have learned in this book. Keep in mind that the earlier you start; the sooner you can start earning passive income from your real estate investments.

Finally, if you enjoyed this book, then I would like to ask you for a favor; would you be kind enough to leave a review for this book on Amazon? It would be greatly appreciated!

Thank you and good luck!